HAL•LEONARD®

VIOLIN PLAY-ALONG

AUDIO ACCESS INCLUDED

Light CLASSICS

CONTENTS

To access audio visit:
www.halleonard.com/mylibrary

Enter Code
1017-9872-1551-9457

ISBN 978-1-4803-5387-9

Jon Vriesacker, Violin
Audio Arrangements by Peter Deneff
Produced and Recorded by Jake Johnson at Paradyme Productions

HAL•LEONARD®
CORPORATION
7777 W. BLUEMOUND RD. P.O. BOX 13819 MILWAUKEE, WI 53213

Visit Hal Leonard Online at
www.halleonard.com

Fiddle Faddle

By Leroy Anderson

Hymn a l'amour

Words by Edith Piaf
Music by Marguerite Monnot

Holiday for Strings

By David Rose

8

Mr. Lucky

By Henry Mancini

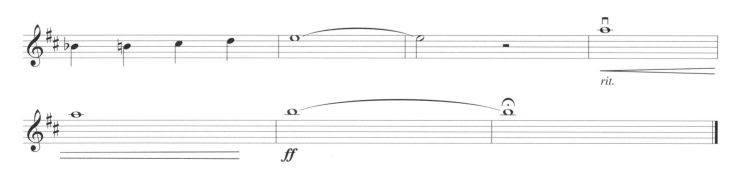

Song from a Secret Garden

By Rolf Lovland

The River Seine
(La Seine)

Words and Music by Allan Roberts and Alan Holt
Original French Text by Flavien Monod and Guy LaFarge

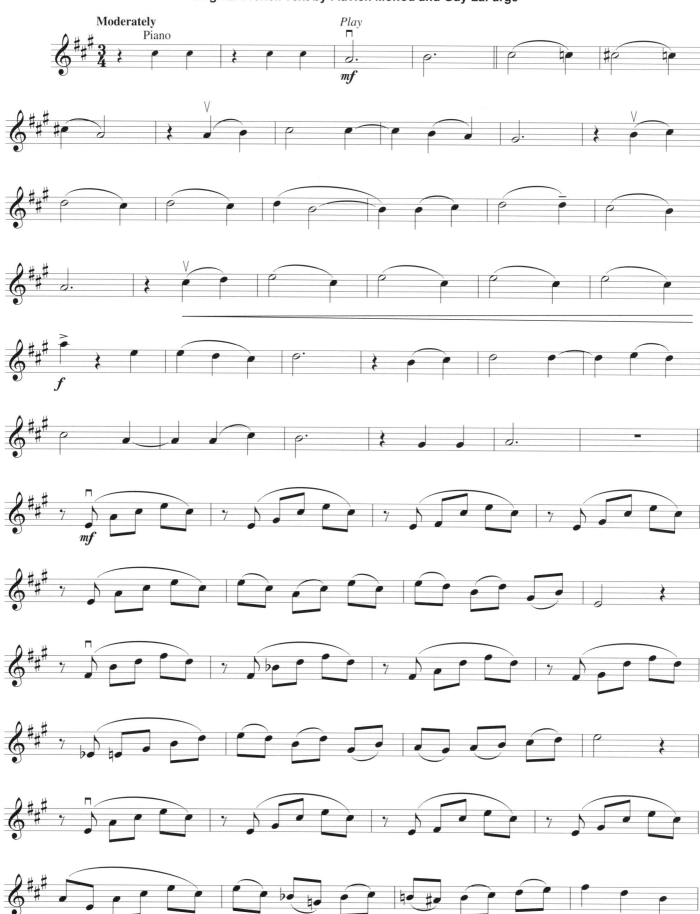

Spartacus – Love Theme

from the Universal-International Picture Release SPARTACUS

By Alex North

rit.

a tempo

rit.

Tara's Theme
(My Own True Love)
from GONE WITH THE WIND

By Max Steiner